STORIES FROM GRANDMA

STORIES *from* GRANDMA

A Fill-In Journal and Family Keepsake

Katie H. Sweeney

ROCKRIDGE PRESS

For general information on our other products and services or to obtain technical support, please contact our Customer Care Department within the United States at (866) 744-2665, or outside the United States at (510) 253-0500.

Rockridge Press publishes its books in a variety of electronic and print formats. Some content that appears in print may not be available in electronic books, and vice versa.

Interior and Cover Designers: Scott Petrower and Carlos Esparza
Art Producer: Samantha Ulban
Editor: Jesse Aylen
Production Manager: Holly Haydash
Production Editor: Melissa Edeburn

All images used under license © Shutterstock.
Author photo courtesy of Jasmin Van T Photography.

ISBN: Print 978-1-63807-360-4
R0

This journal belongs to:

_____

Contents

Introduction
Why You Need to Tell Your Story

As a grandmother, you have an important story to tell. Hearing your unique memories and interesting perspectives not only helps the younger generation better understand their origin, but also guides them on their own life's journey. The only problem is that, with so many life experiences to recount, it's difficult to know where to begin or how to articulate the lessons you'd like to pass down to your children and grandchildren.

Luckily, you've picked up this book. *Stories from Grandma* is a journal meant to help you share your life's narrative with your grandchildren. The details you'll be prompted to describe on each page will give family members a glimpse into where you came from, what you experienced in your life, and what you hope for the future. It's time to think about your feelings, record likes and dislikes, and discover new dreams and wishes. Now is your chance to open up and tell stories and reveal parts of yourself that your children might not even know about. It's an opportunity to describe your past and present and think about—and answer—the questions you regret not asking your own grandmother while she was alive. As you write about your own history, feelings, and thoughts, you will create a legacy that will live on long after you do. This journal will become a treasured family heirloom that will provide meaning for generations to come.

There is no right or wrong way to use this book. Open any page, read the prompt(s), and write as much or as little as you like. Or, start at the beginning and make your way through the chapters sequentially. You may even find it enjoyable to have a grandchild or other family member help you respond to the writing prompts. Dictate your responses while a grandchild scribbles them in the book, or set up a video camera, have family members ask you the questions out loud, and record your answers on audio. Each chapter focuses on a different aspect of your life—from your favorite things to your everyday work to the world events that shaped your outlook. The questions and activities you'll find throughout this journal are meant to trigger memories, highlight personal insights, and help you connect with the younger generations of your family.

Whether you think of your life as grand or humble, ordinary or outstanding, it is an essential part of your children's and grandchildren's heritage, and even the most seemingly mundane memories and ideas can help your loved ones navigate all the unknowns that lie ahead of them.

So just begin—and, most importantly, be yourself!

The process of journaling might surprise you and help you learn things about yourself and your life that you might not have realized before. If something comes to you that doesn't relate to a prompt or question, or you feel like you want to give a longer answer, write it down on the blank pages at the back of the book. Your thoughts, ideas, and memories will serve as inspiration to your family. By filling in these pages, you are creating a blueprint of the past that will be cherished far into the future.

CHAPTER ONE

Who You Are

Although everyone's journey from youth to old age is unique, it all begins the same: with birth. Whether you grew up in the city or the country, in a small apartment or a large house, the first few years of your life were crucial to forming who you are now. In this first chapter, start your journaling experience by sharing the most basic details about who you are. Don't know how to answer a question? Don't worry! This process is meant to be fun and rewarding. Feel free to skip prompts altogether or come back to them later if you like.

YOUR FAMILY TREE

_____
paternal grandmother

_____
paternal grandfather

_____
sibling

_____
sibling

_____
sibling

_____
father

_____
mother

_____
sibling

_____
sibling

_____
maternal grandmother

_____
sibling

_____
maternal grandfather

_____
grandchild

_____
child

_____
grandchild

_____
grandchild

_____
grandchild

_____
child

_____
grandchild

_____
grandchild

_____
child

_____
grandchild

_____
you

_____
grandchild

_____
partner

_____
child

_____
grandchild

_____
partner

_____
grandchild

_____
partner

_____
child

_____
grandchild

_____
partner

_____
grandchild

_____
child

_____
grandchild

_____
grandchild

1. What is your full name?

2. When is your birthday?

3. Where and when were you born?

4. What is the significance of your name?

5. Do you have a nickname? If so, what is it?

6. Who is/was (are/were) your life partner(s)?

7. Were you ever married? If so, what are three things you remember about getting married?

8. What are the names and birthplaces of your children?

9. What is your medical history? Have you overcome any health issues?

10. Name all the places where you have lived.

11. What five adjectives would you use to describe yourself?

CHAPTER TWO

Your Favorite Things

What things have brought you joy over the years? What items instantly put a smile on your face? What objects, places, and people, when you think about them, always cheer you up? Whatever your favorite things are—raindrops on roses, warm woolen mittens, crisp apple strudels—now is the time to share them. Write down whatever comes to mind: any of your favorite things—big, small, and every size in between. The process of identifying what makes you happy will help you get used to the idea of journaling.

What is your favorite color? Why do you love this color? Do you prefer to wear it? Decorate with it? See it in nature?

What is your favorite food and/or drink?

What dessert do you like to have on your birthday?

What is your favorite place to visit? Why?

What is your favorite season, and why?

What is your favorite holiday, and why?

What are your favorite sports or games? If you have any favorite sports teams, have they ever won a championship that seemed unwinnable?

List three of your favorite books.

Who are your favorite musical artists or groups?

List three of your favorite songs.

What types of TV shows or movies do you like to watch?

What do you collect? Records? Artwork? Books? Why do you enjoy collecting these items?

Name three people, dead or alive, fictional or real, who you would like to have dinner with.

If you could be an animal, which animal would you be and why?

If you could have one superpower, what would it be and why?

What makes you laugh?

Which celebrities do you find most attractive, and why?

Who are your role models and heroes?

What is your philosophy about life? What is your motto?

What are your hobbies?

CHAPTER THREE

Family Traditions

In this chapter, you will reflect on family memories from childhood to adulthood. The following prompts are meant to help you reminisce about the past. So take a moment to look back at your life and all that you have accomplished. If you think you haven't accomplished much, think again! You raised a family and are now a grandmother. That is something to be very proud of!

What language did you learn first? What language(s) did your parents speak? How many languages do you speak?

Where are your ancestors from?

What ethnicity do you identify with?

What are your religious and spiritual beliefs and practices?

Share a favorite story that was passed down to you from your parent(s), grandparent(s), or other family member(s).

Do you know any stories about the history of your family name or the origins of your family?

Did your family go on vacation? If so, where? What did you do there?

When someone passed away, how did you honor their life and memory?

In which ways are you like your parents, and in which ways are you different?

_____

_____

_____

_____

_____

What are some of your important family values, and how do you put them into practice?

_____

_____

_____

_____

_____

What is a tradition that you've stopped practicing but wish you could bring back? Why?

What traditions do you want your family to continue after you are gone?

How do you ring in the New Year—quietly at home with family, or with a night out on the town? What do you eat and drink?

What food do you like to have for special family dinners?

Write down a story that you have told many times in your life but never gets old.

What is one ritual you've practiced your whole life and continue to do today?

What is the funniest family story that you remember?

When you were growing up, how did your family celebrate birthdays?

What holidays do you regularly celebrate? How do you celebrate them?

What are the qualities that you most value in a person?

CHAPTER FOUR

Growing Up

Although it's probably been a long time since you were a child, there are most likely plenty of things you remember about your life as a little kid. Maybe you remember the order you picked up from the butcher every week for your mother or the songs that you sang with the high school choir or the name of the shoe store where you and your older sister worked. Whatever comes to mind, jot it down. Return to your childhood home in your mind and see if you can recall what your day-to-day life was like back then.

What do you remember most about your mother?

_____

_____

_____

_____

_____

_____

What do you remember most about your father?

_____

_____

_____

_____

_____

_____

What were your parents' occupations? Did they enjoy their work?

What do you remember most about your grandparents?

Which family member were you closest to? What made you feel closest to them?

What was your childhood like?

What did you enjoy doing as a teen?

What hardships did you overcome as a child or teenager?

Did you ever get into trouble as a teenager? What happened?

Describe your first kiss.

Did you have a pet? If so, what kind of animal was it and what was its name?

What types of chores did you do as a child?

Did you get an allowance? How much was it?

Describe a typical day in your childhood.

What games did you like to play when you were young?

What did your first home look like?

Who lived in your childhood home?

_____

_____

_____

_____

_____

_____

Did you have your own bedroom? Describe your space.

_____

_____

_____

_____

_____

_____

Do you know how much your parents paid for rent or mortgage?

Did you learn how to drive? If so, who taught you, and what do you remember about the experience? If not, how did you get from one place to another?

CHAPTER FIVE

School Days and Life Lessons

Whether you stopped attending school after the eighth grade or have a graduate degree from a prestigious university, you've learned many things throughout your life. You certainly must know a lot! Here is your chance to share your wisdom with the generations to come. If these questions seem tough to answer, take a deep breath: Your perspective, experience, and advice matter. Don't be afraid to share things that your family might not know about you. There is no time like the present to reveal something extraordinary about your past.

Where did you go to school? Write a list of all of the schools you attended (or the ones you remember), from preschool to graduate programs.

What was a valuable life lesson you learned, in or out of the classroom?

What type of student were you? Did you get good grades or barely pass? Did you enjoy homework or hate it?

What were your best and worst subjects in school?

Did you play any sports or instruments or participate in school activities? What did you enjoy?

If you could enroll in a university or college today, what would you study?

Did you have a favorite teacher or a person you looked up to who played an essential role in shaping your life?

What did you want to be when you grew up?

What's the highest honor or award you've ever received? How did you feel about receiving the award?

Have you served your country in the military? When and where?

What's the best advice you were ever given?

Have you ever been involved in a tragic event? What happened?
What life lessons did you learn from overcoming this hardship?

Life is full of tough decisions. Describe a time when you had to make a big decision, and write about what happened afterward.

Was there any single event that drastically changed the course of your life?

What was the scariest thing you ever experienced?

Describe a stressful experience that you overcame.

Do you have any major regrets?

_____

_____

_____

_____

_____

_____

_____

What are some good habits that you developed early on in life?

_____

_____

_____

_____

_____

_____

What things or habits have you quit in your lifetime? Why did you quit them?

What is something that you would love to learn how to do?

CHAPTER SIX

Friends and Family

What would life be without someone to laugh with? Someone to cry with? Someone to cheer you up when you're down? Someone who finishes your sentences and celebrates your birthday with you? Friends and family members are important characters in your personal story. In this chapter, you'll be prompted to remember the friends who brought joy and color to your journey. Think back on the good times and bad times. Can you recall who stood by your side? Your family will enjoy reading your stories and learning more about your insights on relationships.

Who is/was your best friend, and how many years have you known or did you know each other?

_____

_____

_____

_____

_____

What do/did you like most about your best friend?

_____

_____

_____

_____

_____

_____

_____

Who was your first love? How did you know you were in love?

Who is the greatest love of your life, and what qualities first attracted you to this person?

If you could switch places for one day with a relative or friend, who would it be and why?

When did you find out you were going to be a parent for the first time? How did you feel?

What do you enjoy most about being a mother, and what do you enjoy most about being a grandmother?

How would you describe your parenting style? Looking back, is there anything that you would change?

How is being a mother different from being a grandmother, and vice versa?

Who is your oldest friend? How long have you known each other?

If they have passed on, when, where, and how did your parents die? If they are still alive, how old are they now and what is most vibrant about them to you?

What activities do you enjoy doing by yourself? Do you mind spending time alone? For example, would you go to the movies or a restaurant alone?

What do you talk about with your friends? What is the most important reason you stay in touch with your friends? How do you keep in contact? Do you call, exchange text messages, email, or write letters?

Have you ever met a person and instantly became friends? Who was it? Why do you think you connected so immediately?

Are you competitive with your friends and family? In what ways do you compete with them?

Have you ever helped a friend when they were in extreme need? What did you do for your friend, and what was the outcome?

Has a friend ever helped you when you were in desperate need?
Who was that friend and how did they change your perspective on
what friendship means?

Is age important in a friendship? Have you ever had friends who
were older or younger than you? How did the age difference affect
your relationship?

Are you friends with any past loves? Do you think it's possible to be friends with an ex-lover? If you have past loves with whom you are friends, how have they contributed to your life?

Are there any long-lost friends you wish you could reconnect with?

CHAPTER SEVEN

The World You Grew Up In

You have lived through some monumental and memorable moments in history. In this chapter, you'll explore the major global events that have impacted your life. Maybe you experienced these happenings firsthand by fighting in a war or marching for equal rights. Perhaps you witnessed them from afar by reading about them in a newspaper or listening to a radio or television report. Whatever your connection is to important past events, share it. Reading your thoughts and perspectives about these pivotal life events will give your loved ones a richer understanding of history. From the first moon landing to the birth of computers, no event is too big or too small. If it impacted you in any way, write it down.

What are some major national and world events (such as presidential elections and historical firsts) that happened in your lifetime?

Describe one major event that happened in your past but still affects you today.

Have you lived through any significant natural disasters? What happened, and how did you survive?

What is the most life-altering innovation or event that happened during your lifetime? The nuclear bomb? The Internet? A major war?

What political or social cause do you support, and why?

What do you consider the most significant inventions of your lifetime?

What do you think about modern-day technology? Love it or hate it?

How would you describe today's younger generation? In what ways are they different from people in your generation?

What do you miss most about your past? Was it truly the "good old days," or do you prefer the present time?

If you could change one thing about the world today, what would it be?

What do you love most about the world of today? Why?

What causes matter most to you? Health care? Shelter for the homeless? Combating corruption?

_____

_____

_____

_____

_____

_____

What world leaders do you admire? Why?

_____

_____

_____

_____

_____

_____

_____

Is there any time in your life that you remember more vividly than others? What is that time and why is it so memorable?

If you had the power to solve one of the world's problems, what would it be and why?

If you won a billion dollars tomorrow, what would you do with the money?

What's one thing you've always wanted but still don't have?

Today, society is moving to become more inclusive. Which group(s) do you think had it toughest when you were growing up?

What parts of modern life do you just not understand?

CHAPTER EIGHT

Your Job

The average person spends more than 90,000 hours (roughly ⅓ of their life) working. What you did or do professionally has played an essential part in shaping who you are. The environment in which you worked, how you worked, and who you worked with had a tremendous effect on your life. Whether you spent your time in a formal office working as the CEO of a big corporation, passed your days in a busy factory as a blue-collar worker, or worked in a stay-at-home capacity, your career matters. Answer the following prompts to share the story of your working life with your family.

What career aspirations did you have when you were young?
What did you end up doing?

What was your first job, and how did it feel when you began
doing it?

How many different jobs have you had in your lifetime? What were they? If you worked outside of the home, which companies did you work for? If you worked within your home, what were some challenges you faced?

Of all the jobs you've had, which one did you enjoy the most and which one did you enjoy the least? Why?

Did you ever quit or get fired from a job? What happened?

Did you ever change career paths? Why? What career did you leave, and which one did you pursue instead?

What job would you like to have now if you could start over in your career?

What was the biggest challenge you faced in your working life? Did other people from your generation face the same problem?

What kind of big and small decisions did you make throughout your career?

_____

_____

_____

_____

_____

_____

What skills and credentials were necessary for you to perform your job to the best of your ability?

_____

_____

_____

_____

_____

_____

_____

Did your profession require any lifestyle changes? Did you have to travel frequently or move your family to a specific place? Did you need to work nights? Describe how these changes affected your family life.

If you were a young person in today's world, do you think you would choose the same career as you did when you were younger?

What professional organizations or groups have you been a member of? What did you like and/or dislike about these groups? If you didn't belong to any, do you wish you had? Why or why not?

Describe a typical workday at the height of your career. How long was it? What did your daily agenda look like?

Did you have a professional mentor? If so, who was it? If not, what would you have liked to learn from such a person?

Were you able to retire? If so, at what age?

If you were able to retire, how have you enjoyed retirement? What have you done to pass your time?

If you were to go back to work tomorrow, what would you want to do? Why?

Have you participated in any sort of community service or philanthropic efforts? What motivated you to give back?

How do you feel about the career choices you made? Looking back on your professional life, would you consider it a success? Why or why not?

CHAPTER NINE

You and Me

By now, I hope you've gotten the hang of journaling and have developed a rhythm to answering these questions. You've talked about friends, the world you lived in, and your profession. Here you will focus on your relationship with your family. Don't shy away from your feelings. It's okay to discuss difficult things, like what you are afraid of or how hard it was to care for a sick loved one. It's also okay to talk about wonderful things, like how you've managed to find joy in each day and the big and small personal accomplishments you are especially proud of.

What do you remember about the days your children and grandchildren were born or otherwise entered your life? List one to three details you remember about the day each of your children and grandchildren came into your world.

What is your most treasured family memory?

Which traits do you think are the most common in your family?

How would you explain your family to a stranger?

_____

_____

_____

_____

_____

_____

What are the most challenging and most rewarding things about growing older?

_____

_____

_____

_____

_____

What's the best gift you've ever received? Who gave it to you? The gift doesn't have to be a material possession—it could also be advice or experience.

What is your secret to happiness?

As you look back on your life, can you identify any major turning points—milestones or significant events or situations that changed the direction of your personal journey?

What can your grandchildren do to avoid having regrets later in life?

What chores or rules did your parents give you that you chose not to impose on your children and grandchildren?

What sacrifices did you make for your family? Were the sacrifices worth it? What was the outcome?

Have you ever had to care for a sick loved one? What lessons have you learned from that experience?

What is your greatest fear for your family? What is the worst thing that could happen to your loved ones?

What could you tell your family today that they would be surprised to learn about you?

What valuable lessons did your parents or grandparents teach you that are important for the younger generations in your family to remember?

What advice do you have for your children and grandchildren about being in a committed long-term relationship or marriage?

What advice do you have for your children and grandchildren about being a parent?

What makes you proud of your children and grandchildren?

What's the best compliment that your children and grandchildren could give you?

Which family member do you have the most in common with today? Has that changed over time? Why?

CHAPTER TEN

Your Hopes for the Future

Congratulations! You've made it to the last chapter of this journal, and now it's time to focus on the future. Dreaming about the days to come is human nature and something that you can do at any point in life, no matter how old you may be. The following prompts will help you reflect on the past, think about how you feel in the present moment, and imagine what your future and the future of your loved ones will look like.

What haven't you done yet that you would love to do in the future? Do you have any unrealized dreams?

List three things you would like to do with your family in the next six months.

How do you see the world in 10 years?

What are your dreams for your children and grandchildren?

What are your hopes for the future of the planet?

What do you see as your legacy?

In your life, what has defined you? Your experiences? Your values? The relationships you've had with loved ones? The places you have explored? Why?

If you could go back and change something in your life, what would it be?

What are your goals for the future? What do you hope to achieve in the time that is left in your life?

What do you want your family to accomplish when you are gone?

Name one way in which the world has changed to become a better place.

What do you think will be the biggest challenge facing your grandchildren?

What sort of things do you believe are next for humankind? Space travel? Artificial intelligence? Flying cars?

If your life was made into a movie after you passed, which actor would you want to portray you? Why? What would the film focus on?

Which major corporations, technologies, and gadgets will become obsolete by the time your grandchildren are your age? Why?

If you won a billion dollars the day before you die, what would you want your family to do with the money? Why?

How do you feel about death? Are you afraid of it? Why or why not?

Which values (lessons from life experiences, etc.) do you hope your family will inherit from you? Honesty? Work ethic?

What would you tell your grandchildren to acquire/preserve to pass down to future generations?

How do you want your family to remember you?

Additional Questions

Sharing memories with your family is part of a lifelong process. Now that you have created a keepsake with the fill-in journal *Stories from Grandma*, here are more questions that you can use as prompts to create another journal or have meaningful conversations with your family. You may also consider other complementary activities like recording your answers on audio as an additional keepsake that your family will cherish for generations to come.

What sort of things or activities bring you joy? When are you most happy?

What's the most fantastic thing that's happened in your life?

Many believe that age is just a number. What age do you feel you are? Why?

What do you remember about your 20s, 30s, 40s, 50s, and 60s? What events stand out in your mind? How was each decade different from the one before it?

If you could go back to any age, which age would it be and why?

What was the make, model, and color of your family car?

What was it like growing up with siblings? If you didn't have siblings, what do you think it would have been like if you did?

What did you want most as a child but never got?

Who or what influenced your taste and style as a teenager?

Have you gone through any difficult or stressful situations or times in your life that have taught you valuable lessons? If so, describe the situations and write about what you learned from them.

What was your opinion of college? Did you want to go? If so, where and why?

Did you ever experience peer pressure? What happened, and how did you cope with the situation?

What golden rules do you live by?

What do you know now that you wish you had known when you were young?

What are you most thankful for?

What are you most proud of?

How did you meet the love of your life?

Did you ever experience love at first sight? What happened with this person?

What advice did your parents or grandparents give you that you still practice and remember today?

Do your children and grandchildren currently look after you or take care of you? Do you want them to?

Do you think your family is grateful for the impact you have had on their lives?

What does the word "old" mean to you?

Does life seem more complicated now or simpler?

How do you think it will be for future generations?

If you gave birth to your child/children, what was your birth experience like? If they came into your life another way, what was that experience like?

How did you feel as a new mother?

What stage of raising a child was your favorite?

What was the hardest thing about being a mother?

ADDITIONAL NOTES

About the Author

Katie H. Sweeney is a San Francisco–based journalist and modern-day renaissance woman. She has created captivating and original content for some of the Web's leading brands, including *Forbes Travel Guide*, *MyDomaine*, and *PopSugar*. In her spare time, she enjoys crafting delicious meals for her family and friends. Learn more about Katie at KatieHSweeney.com, and follow her culinary adventures on Instagram at @sweenkatcooks.

CPSIA information can be obtained
at www.ICGtesting.com
Printed in the USA
JSHW011619221121
20686JS00002B/10